Dream!

WILL YOU COME ALIVE IN 2025?

WILL YOU COME ALIVE IN 2025?

Richard A. Martin Jr.

PUBLISHING
& associates

Copyright

Unless otherwise indicated, all Scripture quotations are taken from the New King James Version of the Bible, copyright © 1979, 1980, 1982, Thomas Nelson, Inc., Publishers.
All Scripture quotations marked KJV are taken from the King James Version of the Bible.

WILL YOU COME ALIVE IN 2025?
PRINT: ISBN: 978-1-944566-71-5
eBook: ISBN: ISBN: 978-1-944566-72-2

Copyright © 2025 Richard A. Martin Jr.

Bush Publishing & Associates, LLC books may be ordered at everywhere and at *Amazon.com*
For further information, please contact:
Bush Publishing & Associates
Tulsa, Oklahoma
www.bushpublishing.com

Printed in the United States of America.
No portion of this book may be used or reproduced by any means: graphic, electronic, or mechanical, including photocopying, recording, taping, or by any information storage retrieval system, without the written permission of the publisher, except in the case of brief quotations embodied in critical articles and reviews.

Introduction

This book is intended to encourage you to pursue your dreams and goals, and it will give you step by step instructions to achieve them. If you want to achieve your goals and dreams, it is imperative that you follow these instructions.

Jeremiah 29:11 says, "For I know the thoughts that I think toward you, saith the LORD, thoughts of peace, and not of evil, to give you an expected end" (KJV).

The Lord made you dream and planned those things you see in your dreams to do. It is up to you to fulfill those plans and dreams, and as you take the steps of faith to do them, the Lord will do his part and you will have your dreams.

Mark 11:24 affirms, "Therefore I say unto you,

What things soever ye desire, when ye pray, believe that ye receive them, and ye shall have them" (KJV).

Turn those dreams, goals, and desires into reality in 2025.

We have just experienced a huge victory in our presidential elections, the house, and senate seats across the nation.

It is time to step up and achieve our goals. As we pray for the nation and its goals, we can experience our own goals and dreams being fulfilled.

Table of Contents

Introduction ix
Chapter One 3
Chapter Two 9
Chapter Three 19
Chapter Four 27
Chapter Five 33
Chapter Six 41
Chapter Seven 49
Chapter Eight 57
About the Author 61
Resources 63

ONE

DREAM

Chapter One

Dream big in 2025. You might say, "How? I have not dreamed in years. I am too busy to dream. I used to have dreams, but life happens, and now I just work wherever I can get a job and have forgotten what it is like to dream."

That is the first thing you have to fix. How do you fix that? What is a dream? A dream is that thing you always wanted to do, such as own your own business, become a school teacher, drive a semi truck, start your own daycare, visit the world, preach to thousands, or go back to college.

It could be something like owning your own home, your own rental houses, or your own rental offices. It could be having your own kids, having a large farm or a hobby farm, owning a debt-free vehicle, paying off your credit cards, or paying off your house.

Many people call it a bucket list, New Year's resolution, or something of that nature. This is a list of things you have always wanted to do, but life seems to get in the way, so you don't get them done.

The first thing you need to do in order to head in the direction of getting this done is get out a pen and notebook. Yes, it is that simple! Get out a pen and a notebook and start writing.

Write down five to ten things (keep it no more than ten or you will get overwhelmed and lose track. This will lead to not fulfilling the dreams and goals). Find a picture for each goal that supports the vision. Our minds work in pictures, if you think about it. When I say, "Cat," your mind automatically brings up a picture of a short four-legged furry animal that says, "Meow!" If I say, "Snake," your mind automatically has a picture of a long, slender, scaly creature that slithers along the ground. So, find a picture for each goal you have. Put the picture that supports that goal next to the text.

Look at the following examples of a goal list with pictures:

1. Go back to college and earn my degree.

2. Own a daycare.

3. Own a trucking company.

4. Lose weight.

5. Travel to the Grand Canyon.

Put these goals with pictures in front of your eyes and keep them in your mind at least once per day—two or three times per day is better. Read the goals and look at the associated pictures. This will get it drilled into your mind and spirit. This is the first step to achieving your goals for the year.

TWO

REACH
YOUR
GOALS

Chapter Two

Now that you have set your goals and put pictures in front of your eyes, it is time to reach those goals.

Start at the first goal. For example, I will use the goals listed in the last chapter. We will break them down, starting with goal one.

In the previous chapter, goal one was to go back to college and get a degree. Now that we have established that as a goal, we will start taking steps toward achieving that goal.

Goal one, step one: We need to start searching for colleges and universities that offer the degree in which we are seeking and that have an affordable tuition cost.

Step two: Decide which college you want to take your classes through, and if you will do online or attend in-person classes.

Step three: Reach out to that college and fill out an application.

Step four: Find out what programs that college or university offers for financial assistance. Decide how much money you can invest out of pocket or monthly to support the college program that you are taking. I highly recommend using the website *https://forwardfinancialgroup.com/*. Forward Financial Group is a company that has over 30 years of experience, and they specialize in helping people out of debt. They also will help you plan your financial future. This is a great company with great people.

Step five: Start taking classes. Budget your time in a manner that will allow you time to do the classes. It is possible, but sometimes it takes a lot of discipline in budgeting your time.

Goal achieved!

Goal two: Start your own daycare.

Step one: Reach out to your state and get information on daycare requirements in your state.

Step two: Find a building or facility that meets the requirements for daycare.

Step three: Fill out the necessary applications.

Step four: Prepare the building to begin operations.

Step five: Start interviewing potential employees and helpers to help you run the daycare.

Step six: Advertise your daycare to let people know it is coming soon.

Step seven: Get your daycare license hung on the wall in the daycare.

Step eight: Start taking in children.

Goal achieved!

Goal three: Own your own trucking company.

Step one: Make sure you have the proper drivers license. If you need help with that, you can contact Richard's CDL Training via text message at 928-715-2844 or email at *richardscdltraining@gmail.com*.

Step two: Decide what you want to name your company.

Step three: Contact your state and establish the name of your company.

Step four: Establish a bank account under the company name.

Step five: Get a hold of the Federal Motor Carrier association and get a DOT number assigned to your company.

Step six: Shop for a truck that will meet your needs.

Step seven: Decide what type of cargo you wish to transport.

Step eight: Find a trailer designed to transport the type of cargo you plan to transport.

Step nine: Register your truck and trailer with your county and get the proper license tags.

Step ten: Find cargo to start transporting; there are many online freight finding apps you can get to help you find freight.

Step eleven: Start hauling freight!

Goal achieved!

Goal four: Lose weight.

Step one: Decide how much weight you want to lose.

Step two: decide what weight loss program you want to use—there are many out there.

Step three: Set aside time in your day to keep yourself on track with your weight loss program.

Step four: Invest in yourself and feed yourself with encouraging words such as (read this out loud to yourself), "I can do all things through Christ which strengtheneth me" (Philippians 4:13, KJV) or "That the God of our Lord Jesus Christ, the Father of glory, may give unto you the spirit of wisdom and revelation in the knowledge of him: The eyes of your understanding being enlightened; that ye may know what is the hope of his calling, and what the riches of the glory of his inheritance in the saints, and what is the exceeding greatness of his power to us-ward who believe, according to the working of his mighty power, which he wrought in Christ, when he raised him from the dead, and set him at his own right hand in the heavenly places, far above all principality, and power, and might, and dominion, and every name that is named, not only in this world, but also in that which is to come: and hath put all things under his feet, and gave him to be the head over all things to the church, which is his body, the fullness of him that filleth all in all" (Ephesians 1:17–23, KJV). You can also use Ephesians 3:14–21, which says, "For this cause I bow my knees unto the Father of our Lord Jesus Christ, of whom the whole family in heaven and earth is named, that he would grant you, according to the riches of his glory, to be strengthened with might by his Spirit in the inner man; that Christ may dwell in your hearts by faith; that ye, being rooted and grounded in love, may be able to comprehend with all saints what is the breadth, and length, and depth, and height; and to know the love of Christ, which passeth knowledge, that ye might be filled with all the fullness of God. Now unto him that is able to do exceeding abundantly above all that we ask or think, according to the power that worketh in us, unto him be glory in the church by Christ Jesus throughout all ages, world without end. Amen."

Step five: Keep it up every day and don't miss a day.

Goal achieved!

Goal five: Travel to the Grand Canyon.

Step one: Decide how you wish to travel there. Will you drive, fly, ride the train, ride a bus, bike, or walk?

Step two: Figure out how much it will cost to travel in the way you have decided to travel and how long it will take to get there.

Step three: Decide how long you wish to stay and where you will lodge.

Step four: Find out how much it will cost to make this trip.

Step five: Start delegating funding for the trip. If you want something bad enough, you will find the money to do it. Where there is a will or a want to do something, there is a way.

Step six: Travel to the Grand Canyon.

Goal achieved!

All goals and dreams can be achieved in this manner. You just have to set your mind to doing it and follow the steps required to meet that goal.

THREE

MAKE
IT
A
HABIT

Chapter Three

Schedule the time of day you will work toward your dreams and goals.

Like any habit, success doesn't come by only doing it once. If you go to the gym once and don't go back the next time you are supposed to, it will be easy to stop going all together. If you continue to go to the gym every day for several days or weeks, it becomes a habit that your body can not do without. Your body desires to go to the gym every day.

If you go to church one time and don't go back, it is easy to just stop going all together, but if you go over and over again, you crave it and it becomes a part of who you are.

If you smoke a cigarette one time and don't smoke

anymore, it is easy to quit. If you smoke every day, your body begins to crave it and it is hard to quit doing it.

If you read the bible once in a while, it is easy to quit. If you read the bible every day, you crave it and it becomes a habit. It is just something you do.

It is important that we make the goals and dreams we have a part of who we are so that we just do it without thinking about it.

Habits are built by repetition. Satan knows this, and that is why he always tries to get us to do bad things over and over again. When we do this, it sears our conscience to not recognize it as wrong, and so it becomes a part of who we are. That is why criminals have a hard time breaking the cycle when they have done wrong; they get punished for it, yet they do it again and again. That is because it is such a habit to them that they can't seem to break it no matter how hard they try.

1 Timothy 4:1–2 reads, "Now the Spirit speaketh expressly, that in the latter times some shall depart from the faith, giving heed to seducing spirits, and doctrines of devils; speaking lies in hypocrisy; having their conscience seared with a hot iron…"

When we make our dreams and goals our habits, they just happen naturally. We don't think about it—we just do it.

Being kind to others is a natural habit that we have when we are kids. Most kids are naturally kind to others. It is only when the things they hear and see every day go against that that it becomes a habit to be mean and thus sears their conscience against the kindness they were born with. This is why they start rebelling and doing bad things. Now, yes, there is a certain sense of rebellion that they are born with because they are flesh and flesh is part of this world's cursed system. It is by listening to and feeding on the right things that kindness comes out and is dominant. This is why it is so important to be deliberate about what things you are watching, doing, and listening to. Your kids are watching you and learning from you.

Make your goals and dreams the habit of your life. Repeat the good things you want for your life when it is hard to do so, and those things will become your life.

What is in me that has become a habit? Your words will identify where you are in this process. Matthew 12:33–37 (KJV) notes, "Either make the tree good, and his fruit good; or else make the tree corrupt, and his fruit corrupt: for the tree is known by his fruit. O generation of vipers, how can ye, being evil, speak good things? for out of the abundance of the heart the mouth speaketh. A good man out of the good treasure of the heart bringeth forth good things: and an evil man out of the evil treasure bringeth forth evil things. But I say unto you, That every idle word that men shall speak, they shall give account thereof in the day of judgment. For by thy words thou shalt be justified, and by thy words thou shalt be condemned."

Our words are either for us or against us. How do I know where I am in this area? When you walk out to your car and you have a flat tire, what comes out of your mouth? Is it cussing, cursing, throwing a temper tantrum, and kicking the tire? Or is it, "Praise God, I have a spare tire, so I can at least change it and go on about my business"?

When you smash your finger with a hammer, a door, or a heavy object, what comes out of your mouth? Is it cussing, cursing, throwing a temper tantrum, and hitting things? Or is it, "Praise God, I can feel my finger and I know it is hurt"? Because some people don't have any feeling in their fingers and may not even know they are hurt, you are blessed that you can feel the pain. Just step back and praise God that you can.

1 Thessalonians 5:15–23 (KJV) reads, "See that none render evil for evil unto any man; but ever follow

that which is good, both among yourselves, and to all men. Rejoice evermore. Pray without ceasing. In every thing give thanks: for this is the will of God in Christ Jesus concerning you. Quench not the Spirit. Despise not prophesyings. Prove all things; hold fast that which is good. Abstain from all appearance of evil. And the very God of peace sanctifies you wholly; and I pray to God your whole spirit and soul and body be preserved blameless unto the coming of our Lord Jesus Christ."

Philippians 4:4–7 (KJV) also says, "Rejoice in the Lord always: and again I say, rejoice! Let your moderation be known unto all men. The Lord is at hand. Be careful for nothing; but in every thing by prayer and supplication with thanksgiving let your requests be made known unto God. And the peace of God, which passeth all understanding, shall keep your hearts and minds through Christ Jesus."

When things get hard, are you speaking negatively and saying the thing which you see, or are you speaking the things you want to see? Mark 11:22 reads, "And Jesus answering saith unto them, 'Have faith in God. For verily I say unto you, That whosoever shall say unto this mountain, Be thou removed, and be thou cast into the sea; and shall not doubt in his heart, but shall believe that those things which he saith shall come to pass; he shall have whatsoever he saith. Therefore I say unto you, What things soever ye desire, when ye pray, believe that ye receive them, and ye shall have them" (KJV).

Are you praising God for what you don't have? We will talk more about this aspect in chapter eight of this book.

It is up to you to create the habits you want in your life. Step up to the plate and begin the repetition process to attain the habits that create the dreams and goals you want in your life.

FOUR

DELEGATE YOUR TIME

Chapter Four

Find the time in your day to read the bible and read the visions and dreams you have put on paper with pictures. Behold those things with your eyes every day. Whether that means getting up earlier to do it or doing it before bed at night. If you do it both morning and night, you will see quicker results.

It is your time to delegate according to what you want to achieve in life. Are you going to spend your whole life working for other people, helping them achieve their goals and dreams in life, or are you going to step out and achieve your goals and dreams?

Now, don't get me wrong, it is good to help others

achieve their goals and dreams, and part of the process is working for others helping them to achieve that, but that should not be your whole life.

You need to delegate time to invest in your own goals and dreams with the help of the Lord and his word. Ecclesiastes 3:1–3 says, "To every thing there is a season, and a time to every purpose under the heaven: A time to be born, and a time to die; a time to plant, and a time to pluck up that which is planted; A time to kill, and a time to heal; a time to break down, and a time to build up…" (KJV).

You need to delegate the time to invest in your self-care plan in order to achieve your visions and goals. Spend time every day without fail in the word of God, and also spend time reading and looking at your visions.

Terry Sevelle Foy says to make a vision board. Maybe you need to get a corkboard, print out each vision with the pictures, and pin them on the vision board. You should also get a scripture from the bible to support your self care and pin the scripture on the board along with the vision and pictures.

Go to this board one or two times per day and read everything, taking in the visuals of it. This will soon become a habit, and you will look forward to doing it. Pretty soon, you won't even have to think about doing it. You will just automatically go to that vision board where you can behold these visions and goals with your eyes.

As you make the time to do this, you will start seeing these things come to pass. You should also keep track of your visions and goals by writing down the date and time when you first started the habit of pursuing them. Write down the date and time every time you make progress toward achieving each vision or goal, and write down the date and time when the vision or goal becomes a reality.

Go back to this notebook often to remind yourself of the progress being made. If you start to lose focus or become discouraged, go back to the notebook.

This notebook will help you remember the progress

that has been made as well as provide you with a good testimony as to what God is helping you accomplish.

FIVE

MOTIVATED

Chapter Five

Jeremiah 29:11 says, "For I know the thoughts that I think toward you, saith the LORD, thoughts of peace, and not of evil, to give you an expected end" (KJV).

Mark 11:24 states, "Therefore I say unto you, What things soever ye desire, when ye pray, believe that ye receive them, and ye shall have them" (KJV).

Philippians 4:13 reads, "I can do all things through Christ which strengtheneth me" (KJV), and Ephesians 1:17–23 tells us, "That the God of our Lord Jesus Christ, the Father of glory, may give unto you the spirit of wisdom and revelation in the knowledge of him: The eyes of your understanding being enlightened; that ye may know what is the hope of his calling, and what the riches of the glory of his inheritance in the saints, and what is the exceeding greatness of his power to us-ward who believe, according to the working of his mighty power, which he wrought in Christ, when he raised him from the dead, and set him at his own right hand in the heavenly places, far above all principality, and power, and might, and dominion, and every name that is named, not only in this world, but also in that which is to come: And hath put all things under his feet, and gave him to be the head over all things to the church, which is his body, the fullness of him that filleth all in all" (KJV).

Ephesians 3:14–21 (KJV) asserts, "For this cause I bow my knees unto the Father of our Lord Jesus Christ, of whom the whole family in heaven and earth is named, that he would grant you, according to the riches of his glory, to be strengthened with might by his Spirit in the inner man; that Christ may dwell in your hearts by faith; that ye, being rooted and grounded in love, may be able to comprehend with all saints what is the breadth, and length, and depth, and height; and to know the love of Christ, which passeth knowledge, that ye might be filled with all the fullness of God. Now unto him that is able to do exceeding abundantly above all that we ask or think, according to the power that worketh in us, unto him be glory in the church by Christ Jesus throughout all ages, world without end. Amen."

Romans 10:9–10 proclaims, "That if thou shalt confess with thy mouth the Lord Jesus, and shalt believe in thine heart that God hath raised him from the dead, thou shalt be saved. For with the heart man believeth unto righteousness; and with the mouth confession is made unto salvation" (KJV).

Repeat these confessions out loud so you can hear yourself speaking them.

Confess: "I come to you today, Lord. I thank you for dying on the cross for my sins and rising again on the third day. I ask you to come into my life. Help me to live for you from this day forward. I ask you to help me to live for you. I commit my life and my ways to you today, Lord. In Jesus' name I pray, amen."

Acts 2:1–4 observes, "And when the day of Pentecost was fully come, they were all with one accord in one place. And suddenly there came a sound from heaven as of a rushing mighty wind, and it filled all the house where they were sitting. And there appeared unto them cloven tongues like as of fire, and it sat upon each of them. And they were all filled with the Holy Ghost, and began to speak with other tongues, as the Spirit gave them utterance" (KJV).

Confess: Dear Lord Jesus, I do believe you sent your Holy Spirit to this Earth to give us a heavenly language that is just for us. I thank you that that includes a language specific to you for communications in the Spirit. I thank you for filling me with your Holy Spirit now, and I accept the language that accompanies that Holy Spirit. Please help me to speak that language that my mind doesn't understand but that heaven understands. I receive it now, in Jesus' name, amen." Now, start speaking the language that is coming up in your spirit that your head does not understand.

Acts 17:28 says, "For in him we live, and move, and have our being; as certain also of your own poets have said, For we are also his offspring."

Confess: In Jesus Christ, I live and move and have my being.

John 15:5–7 states, "I am the vine, ye are the branches: He that abideth in me, and I in him, the same bringeth forth much fruit: for without me ye can do nothing. If a man abides not in me, he is cast forth as a branch, and is withered; and men gather them, and cast them into the fire, and they are burned. If ye abide in me, and my words abide in you, ye shall ask what ye will, and it shall be done unto you" (KJV).

Confess: I abide in him. I live in him. He is the vine, I am the branch. The vine is in the branch and the branch in the vine. His life, the life of God, is in me. His nature, the love nature, is in me. Just as blood flows through my natural body, the life and nature of God flows through my inner man.

2 Corinthians 5:17 (KJV) reads, "Therefore if any man be in Christ, he is a new creature: old things have passed away; behold, all things have become new."

Confess: I am a new creature in Christ Jesus. My whole being and life now has the ability and nature of God flowing within it.

Ephesians 2:10 (KJV) remarks, "For we are his workmanship, created in Christ Jesus unto good works, which God hath before ordained that we should walk in them."

Confess: I am his workmanship. I am a new creation in Christ Jesus.

Romans 8:37 (KJV) articulates, "Nay, in all these things we are more than conquerors through him that loved us."

Confess: I am more than a conqueror through

Christ Jesus, who saved me.

Build up your self worth and confidence through finding good scriptures like these and motivate yourself!

SIX

RELATIONSHIPS

Chapter Six

Building a healthy relationship with those around you is very important.

I want you to do an assignment using the following example. You're going to write down everything you would want people to say about you if you died today.

1. What would I want people to say about my character?

   _____
   _____
   _____
   _____
   _____
   _____

2. What would I want them to say about my ability to build and maintain healthy relationships?

_____
_____
_____
_____
_____

3. What would I want them to say about my ability to maintain my finances?

_____
_____
_____
_____
_____

4. What would I want them to say about my dreams? Was I a big dreamer that never accomplished anything, or one who always accomplished what I set your mind to?

_____
_____
_____
_____
_____

5. What would I want them to say about my ability to maintain my dates and schedules?

_____
_____
_____
_____
_____

6. What would I want them to say about my ability to be on time for appointments?

   _____
   _____
   _____
   _____
   _____

7. What would I want them to say about my thanks and appreciation?

   _____
   _____
   _____
   _____
   _____

This exercise puts things into perspective and gets you to look at yourself in the eyes of people around you. This is not intended to get you to look down on yourself or make you feel inferior; it is intended to give you a way to recognize areas where you might need improvement.

First and foremost, you need to build healthy relationships with your family and friends.

In building relationships, it is important to remember the names of those whom you are in contact with.

I am a school bus driver and a paraeducator. I always make it a point to greet all my students, their parents, and my coworkers by name every time I see them, and as I drop off my students in the evening, I tell them to have a good evening and call them by name. This not only tells them that you care about them as a person, but it also helps me remember their names. When they know that you care about them for who they are, they will be much more responsive to you when you have to discipline them.

When you build the same relationships with the parents, if discipline issues arise that go far enough for you to have to call the parent about it, they are much more likely to help you with the issue.

The same principle applies to your friends and family. If you are kind and caring to them, they are much more likely to be kind and loving back to you.

Ephesians 4:31–32 tells us, "Let all bitterness, and wrath, and anger, and clamour, and evil speaking, be put away from you, with all malice: and be ye kind one to another, tenderhearted, forgiving one another, even as God for Christ's sake hath forgiven you."

Matthew 7:12 also says, "So then, whatever you desire that others would do to and for you, even so do also to and for them, for this is (sums up) the Law and the Prophets" (AMPC).

Always treat others as you would have them treat you. If you invest in healthy actions and relationships with others, it will always come back to you.

Luke 6:38 reads, "For if you give, you will get! Your gift will return to you in full and overflowing measure, pressed down, shaken together to make room for more, and running over. Whatever measure you use to give—large or small—will be used to measure what is given back to you" (TLB).

Show others love and kindness in all things. Building relationships with others and as you do you will see to many of your own goals and dreams coming true just by default.

1 Corinthians 13:4–8 professes, "Love endures long and is patient and kind; love never is envious nor boils over with jealousy, is not boastful or vainglorious, does not display itself haughtily. It is not conceited (arrogant and inflated with pride); it is not rude (unmannerly) and does not act unbecomingly. Love (God's love in us) does not insist on its own rights or its own way, for it is not self-seeking; it is not touchy or fretful or resentful; it takes no account of the evil done to it [it pays no attention to a suffered wrong]. It does not rejoice at injustice and unrighteousness, but rejoices when right and truth prevail. Love bears up under anything and everything that comes, is ever ready to believe the best of every person, its hopes are fadeless under all

circumstances, and it endures everything [without weakening]. Love never fails [never fades out or becomes obsolete or comes to an end]. As for prophecy (the gift of interpreting the divine will and purpose), it will be fulfilled and pass away; as for tongues, they will be destroyed and cease; as for knowledge, it will pass away [it will lose its value and be superseded by truth]" (AMPC).

As you build these relationships, you will see things work out for you!

SEVEN

FINANCIAL INVESTMENTS

Chapter Seven

Everyone knows it takes money to accomplish our dreams and goals on top of our will, time, and drive.

We must set our mind to budgeting our finances as well as the other things. Concerning our money, let's look to Malachi 3:6–11 for wisdom. It reads, "For I am the Lord, I do not change; that is why you, O sons of Jacob, are not consumed. Even from the days of your fathers you have turned aside from My ordinances and have not kept them. Return to me, and I will return to you, says the Lord of hosts. But you say, How shall we return? Will a man rob or defraud God? Yet you rob and defraud Me. But you say, In what way do we rob or defraud You? [You have withheld your] tithes and offerings. You are cursed with the curse, for you are robbing Me, even this whole nation. Bring all the tithes (the whole tenth of your income) into the storehouse, that there may be food in My house, and prove Me now by it, says the Lord of hosts, if I will not open the windows of heaven for you and pour you out a blessing, that there shall not be room enough to receive it. And I will rebuke the devourer [insects and plagues] for your sake and he shall not destroy the fruits of your ground, neither shall your vine drop its fruit before the time in the field, says the Lord of hosts" (AMPC).

We must start with 10% of all our increases. This means our income from our jobs, monetary blessings that people may give us, or inheritances we may receive. This also includes the first fruits of our gardens, vineyards, and fields. How do you give that? Well, it is quite simple.

Matthew 6:1–4 proclaims, "Take heed that ye do not your alms before men, to be seen of them: otherwise ye have no reward of your Father which is in heaven. Therefore when thou doest thine alms, do not sound a trumpet before thee, as the hypocrites do in the synagogues and in the streets, that they may have the glory of men. Verily I say unto you, They have their reward. But when thou doest alms, let not thy left hand know what thy right hand doeth: That thine alms may be in secret: and the Father which seeth in secret himself shall reward thee openly" (KJV).

I will start with the way the Lord taught me. I have always given my 10%. My mother taught me to give 10% of all my increase from a young age. I would crawl around, finding change under the carpet corners and in couch cushions, and I would put it in my piggy bank. Mom taught me that 10% of all my increase belongs to the Lord. If I found a dime, then one penny belonged to the Lord. I honored that. If I got ten dollars for Christmas, then one dollar belonged to the Lord. If I got twenty dollars for my birthday, then two dollars belonged to the Lord.

When I started mowing lawns at age 11 and got paid for it, I would automatically put the 10% in the offering at church on Sunday.

When I got older and started working a regular job, I automatically paid my 10% tithe. When I started my own business at age 15, I always paid my tithe.

As I got older, I started learning about offerings, which are financial givings above tithe. This giving brings further blessings on us.

I started giving more in my offerings to help bring the gospel to the world through a ministry I believed in. I began to be blessed with money from unexpected channels. My obedience to give above my tithe opened the door for the unexpected channels to start giving me money and items in which I needed but did not have the funds to get.

I have continued to give this way. One good way to start this type of flow is to start a separate bank account in which you put a certain percentage of your income—not your tithe—into this account. Then, you can pray about how much to give to what cause as an offering. This account is never to be used as an emergency fund in any way, shape, or form! This is strictly funding to give to those in need or to other ministries. If you rob from this account for anything other than helping others (as the Lord directs), you will quickly go broke. If you are careful to only give where the Lord directs, you will never be without seed money.

As for how the Lord taught me about the first fruits of my crops… I garden every year, producing many fruits and vegetables. At first, I struggled for years to get much of a crop. One day, as I was in my garden, I was praying and trying to figure out what was wrong and why I hardly got a crop.

The Lord told me two things. First, He said, "You are eating your seed." I had heard this in the area of finances, but never in reference to my garden plants. I was taken aback for a moment. I said, "Lord, what do you mean?" He said, "The first tomato, the first watermelon, the first pepper, the first cucumber, the first strawberry—they belong to me, and you're eating them."

So, I got the first strawberry and the first tomato

that came off the plant that year and gave it to my neighbor to test things out a little bit. I also gave them the first watermelon. I did not give them the first peppers or cucumbers or anything else—just the tomato, strawberry, and watermelon.

After I did that that year, I could not keep up with my tomato production, my strawberry production, or my watermelon production. I was giving away so much and eating all we could eat and I still had an overflow of those three items. The rest of the garden was sparse.

I said, "Okay Lord, I understand the thing about giving away the first fruits now—I have learned my lesson." The next year, I gave away the first fruits of everything I grew, and I was soon overwhelmed with abundant crops.

The second thing He told me is that the soil was poor quality. Even though I had picked the best soil spot in my yard, He said the soil was bad. I said, "Lord, how do I fix that?" He gave me the idea to make a raised bed and told me exactly how to build the potting planters and how to do the soil.

Doing the soil was a four-step process with different soil types and minerals. He told me exactly where to get each soil type and what order to put the soil in as well as how to mix it.

I did exactly as the Lord told me to do with the planters and the soil on top of sowing the first fruits of everything. After that, I could not keep up, and all my neighbors were asking me how in the world I was growing such a luscious garden. This opened up the opportunity for me to witness to them and tell them how the Lord had instructed me.

That is how the Lord taught me about sowing the first fruit on not just my money, but my goods as well.

If you endeavor to invest your finances and the first fruits of every part of your increase to the Lord, the Lord will continue to increase you.

This works the same way for cattle and livestock. If you give your first fruits every year, you will have abundance you never imagined was possible.

EIGHT

THANKSGIVING

Chapter Eight

One of the most important parts of Thanksgiving is praise. When you start achieving your goals and dreams, it is important to give thanks for every small victory.

If you read Psalms, David danced and praised the Lord in all things. Now David, like all of us in today's world, had struggles. He did not always live and behave in a way that pleased God, but we serve a merciful and gracious God who will take us through anything so long as we praise.

Psalms 145:1–2 (KJV) declares, "I will extol thee, my God, O king; and I will bless thy name for ever and ever. Every day will I bless thee, and I will praise thy name for ever and ever."

Never forget to give thanks to God in all things. Psalm 103:1–5 (KJV) says, "Bless the LORD, O my soul: and all that is within me, bless his holy name. Bless the LORD, O my soul, and forget not all his benefits: Who forgiveth all thine iniquities; who healeth all thy diseases; Who redeemeth thy life from destruction; who crowneth thee with lovingkindness and tender mercies; Who satisfieth thy mouth with good things; so that thy youth is renewed like the eagle's."

It is very important to give thanks. Don't be like the nine lepers who failed to go back and give thanks to God for the great things he had done. Luke 17:11–19 (KJV) tells us, "And it came to pass, as he went to Jerusalem, that he passed through the midst of Samaria and Galilee. And as he entered into a certain village, there met him ten men that were lepers, which stood afar off: And they lifted up their voices, and said, Jesus, Master, have mercy on us. And when he saw them, he said unto them, Go shew yourselves unto the priests. And it came to pass, that, as they went, they were cleansed. And one of them, when he saw that he was healed, turned back, and with a loud voice glorified God, and fell down on his face at his feet, giving him thanks: and he was a Samaritan. And Jesus answering said, 'Were there not ten cleansed? but where are the nine? There are not found that returned to give glory to God, save this stranger.' And he said unto him, 'Arise, go thy way: thy faith hath made thee whole.'"

1 Thessalonians 5:16–18 insists, "Rejoice evermore. Pray without ceasing. In everything give thanks: for this is the will of God in Christ Jesus concerning you.

As you write down your dreams and visions, reach your goals, embrace your habits, delegate your time, motivate yourself through the word of God, build healthy relationships, invest your resources into things you believe in, and don't forget to praise and give thanks in all things, you will achieve your goals and dreams.

Resources

www.kcm.org

www.flcbranson.org

https://forwardfinancialgroup.com/

richardscdltraining@gmail.com

bush
PUBLISHING
& associates

www.ingramcontent.com/pod-product-compliance
Lightning Source LLC
Chambersburg PA
CBHW050043080526
44586CB00014B/1439